Poems on Various Subjects, Religious and Moral. By Phillis Wheatley, Negro Servant to Mr. John Wheatley, of Boston, in New England

PHILLIS WHEATLEY NEGRO SERVANT to M.ʳ JOHN WHEATLEY, of BOSTON.

Published according to Act of Parliament, Sept.ʳ 1.1773 by Arch.ᵈ Bell.

Bookseller N.º 8 near the Saracens Head Aldgate

P O E M S

ON

VARIOUS SUBJECTS,

RELIGIOUS AND MORAL.

BY

PHILLIS WHEATLEY,

NEGRO SERVANT to Mr. JOHN WHEATLEY,
of BOSTON, in NEW ENGLAND.

L O N D O N:

Printed for A. BELL, Bookseller, Aldgate; and sold by
Messrs. COX and BERRY, King-Street, *BOSTON.*

MDCCLXXIII.

Entered at Stationers Hall.

DEDICATION.

To the Right Honourable the

COUNTESS of HUNTINGDON,

THE FOLLOWING

P O E M S

Are moft refpectfully

Infcribed,

By her much obliged,

Very humble,

And devoted Servant,

Phillis Wheatley.

Bofton, June 12,
1773.

PREFACE.

THE following POEMS were written originally for the Amusement of the Author, as they were the Products of her leisure Moments. She had no Intention ever to have published them; nor would they now have made their Appearance, but at the Importunity of many of her best, and most generous Friends; to whom she considers herself, as under the greatest Obligations.

As her Attempts in Poetry are now sent into the World, it is hoped the Critic will not severely censure their Defects; and we presume they have too much Merit

to

to be caſt aſide with Contempt,
as worthleſs and trifling Effuſions.

As to the Diſadvantages ſhe has
laboured under, with Regard to
Learning, nothing needs to be of‐
fered, as her Maſter's Letter in the
following Page will ſufficiently ſhew
the Difficulties in this Reſpect ſhe
had to encounter.

With all their Imperfections, the
Poems are now humbly ſubmitted
to the Peruſal of the Public.

The

The following is a Copy of a LETTER sent by the Author's Master to the Publisher.

PHILLIS was brought from *Africa* to *America*, in the Year 1761, between Seven and Eight Years of Age Without any Assistance from School Education, and by only what she was taught in the Family, she, in fi.teen Months Time from her Arrival, attained the English Language, to which she was an utter Stranger before, to such a Degree, as to read any, the most difficult Parts of the Sacred Writings, to the great Astonishment of all who heard her

As to her WRITING, her own Curiosity led her to it, and this she learnt in so short a Time, that in the Year 1765, she wrote a Letter to the Rev. Mr. Occom, the *Indian* Minister, while in *England*.

She has a great Inclination to learn the Latin Tongue, and has made some Progress in it. This Rea.... g..n by her Master who bought her, and v.th w'u ne now lives.

JOHN WHEATLEY.

Boston, Nov. 14, 1772.

To the PUBLICK.

AS it has been repeatedly fuggefted to the Publifher, by Perfons, who have feen the Manufcript, that Numbers would be ready to fufpect they were not really the Writings of PHILLIS, he has procured the following Atteftation, from the moft refpectable Characters in *Bofton*, that none might have the leaft Ground for difputing their *Original*.

WE whofe Names are under-written, do affure the World, that the POEMS fpecified in the following Page, * were (as we verily believe) written by PHILLIS, a young Negro Girl, who was but a few Years fince, brought an uncultivated Barbarian from *Africa*, and has ever fince been, and now is, under the Difadvantage of ferving as a Slave in a Family in this Town. She has been examined by fome of the beft Judges, and is thought qualified to write them

His Excel ency THOMAS HUTCHINSON, *Governor*,

The Hon ANDREW OLIVER, *Lieutenant-Governor*.

The Hon. Thomas Hubbard,	*The Rev.* Charles Chauncy, D D.
The Hon. John Erving,	*The Rev.* Mather Byles, D. D.
The Hon James Pitts,	*The Rev* Ed Pemberton, D.D.
The Hon Harrifon Gray,	*The Rev* Andrew Elliot, D.D
The Hon. James Bowdoin,	*The Rev* Samuel Cooper, D.D.
John Hancock, *Efq*;	*The Rev. Mr.* Samuel Mather,
Jofeph Green, *Efq*;	*The Rev. Mr* John Moorhead,
Richard Carey, *Efq*,	*Mr* John Wheatley, *her Mafter*.

N. B The original Atteftation, figned by the above Gentlemen, may be feen by applying to *Archibald Bell*, Bookfeller, No 8, *Aldgate-Street*

---

* The Words " *following Page*," allude to the Contents of the Manufcript Copy, which are wrote at the Back of the above Atteftation.

P O E M S

O N

VARIOUS SUBJECTS.

To MÆCEÑAS.

MÆCENAS, you, beneath the myrtle
   shade,
Read o'er what poets sung, and shepherds play'd.
What felt those poets but you feel the same?
Does not your soul possess the sacred flame?
Their noble strains your equal genius shares 5
In softer language, and diviner airs.

 While *Homer* paints lo! circumfus'd in air,
Celestial Gods in mortal forms appear;

B   Swift

Swift as they move hear each recefs rebound,
Heav'n quakes, earth trembles, and the fhores re-
     found.   10
Great Sire of verfe, before my mortal eyes,
The lightnings blaze acrofs the vaulted fkies,
And, as the thunder fhakes the heav'nly plains,
A deep-felt horror thrills through all my veins.
When gentler ftrains demand thy graceful fong, 15
The length'ning line moves languifhing along.
When great *Patroclus* courts *Achilles'* aid,
The grateful tribute of my tears is paid;
Prone on the fhore he feels the pangs of love,
And ftern *Pelides* tend'reft paffions move.   20

   Great *Maro's* ftrain in heav'nly numbers flows,
The *Nine* infpire, and all the bofom glows.
O could I rival thine and *Virgil's* page,
Or claim the *Mufes* with the *Mantuan* Sage;
Soon the fame beauties fhould my mind adorn, 25
And the fame ardors in my foul fhould burn:
Then fhould my fong in bolder notes arife,
And all my numbers pleafingly furprize;
                                        But

But here I fit, and mourn a grov'ling mind,
That fain would mount, and ride upon the wind.

Not you, my friend, thefe plaintive ftrains be-
    come,
Not you, whofe bofom is the *Mufes* home;
When they from tow'ring *Helicon* retire,
They fan in you the bright immortal fire,
But I lefs happy, cannot raife the fong,   35
The fault'ring mufic dies upon my tongue.

The happier *Terence* * all the choir infpir'd,
His foul replenifh'd, and his bofom fir'd,
But fay, ye *Mufes*, why this partial grace,
To one alone of *Afric*'s fable race,   40
From age to age tranfmitting thus his name
With the firft glory in the rolls of fame?

Thy virtues, great *Mæcenas* ! fhall be fung
In praife of him, from whom thofe virtues fprung:

* He was an *African* by birth.

B 2   While

While blooming wreaths around thy temples
    fpread,   45
I'll fnatch a laurel from thine honour'd head,
While you indulgent fmile upon the deed.

   As long as *Thames* in ftreams majeftic flows,
Or *Naiads* in their oozy beds repofe,
While *Phœbus* reigns above the ftarry train,   50
While bright *Aurora* purples o'er the main,
So long, great Sir, the mufe thy praife fhall fing,
So long thy praife fhall make *Parnaffus* ring :
Then grant, *Mæcenas*, thy paternal rays,
Hear me propitious, and defend my lays.   55

On VIRTUE.

O Thou bright jewel in my aim I strive
    To comprehend thee. Thine own words
        declare
Wisdom is higher than a fool can reach.
I cease to wonder, and no more attempt
Thine height t' explore, or fathom thy profound. 5
But, O my soul, sink not into despair,
Virtue is near thee, and with gentle hand
Would now embrace thee, hovers o'er thine head.
Fain would the heav'n-born soul with her converse,
Then seek, then court her for her promis'd bliss.

Auspicious queen, thine heav'nly pinions spread,
And lead celestial *Chastity* along ,
Lo! now her sacred retinue descends,
Array'd in glory from the orbs above.
Attend me, *Virtue*, thro' my youthful years ! 15
O leave me not to the false joys of time !
But guide my steps to endless life and bliss.

                                    Greatness,

Greatneſs, or *Goodneſs*, ſay what l ſhall call thee,
To give an h.gher appellation ſtill,
Teach me a better ſtrain, a nobler lay,   20
O thou, enthron'd with Cherubs in the realms of
     day !

To the University of CAMBRIDGE, in NEW-ENGLAND.

WHILE an intrinfic ardor prompts to write,
 The mufes promife to affift my pen ;
'Twas not long fince I left my native fhore
The land of errors, and *Egyptian* gloom :
Father of mercy, 'twas thy gracious hand   5
Brought me in fafety from thofe dark abodes.

 Students, to you 'tis giv'n to fcan the heights
Above, to traverfe the ethereal fpace,
And mark the fyftems of revolving worlds.
Still more, ye fons of fcience ye receive   10
The blifsful news by meffengers from heav'n,
How *Jefus'* blood for your redemption flows.
See him with hands out-ftretcht upon the crofs;
Immenfe compaffion in his bofom glows ;
He hears revilers, nor refents their fcorn :   15
What matchlefs mercy in the Son of God !
When the whole human race by fin had fall'n,

He

He deign'd to die that they might rife again,
And fhare with him in the fublimeft fkies,
Life without death, and glory without end.   20

Improve your privileges while they ftay,
Ye pupils, and each hour redeem, that bears
Or good or bad report of you to heav'n.
Let fin, that baneful evil to the foul,
By you be fhunn'd, nor once remit your guard,   25
Supprefs the deadly ferpent in its egg.
Ye blooming plants of human race divine,
An *Ethiop* tells you 'tis your greateft foe;
Its tranfient fweetnefs turns to endlefs pain,
And in immenfe perdition finks the foul   30

To

To the K I N G's Moſt Excellent Majeſty.
1768.

YOUR ſubjects hope, dread Sire—
    The crown upon your brows may flouriſh
        long,
And that your arm may in your God be ſtrong!
O may your ſceptre num'rous nations ſway,
And all with love and readineſs obey!

But how ſhall we the *Britiſh* king reward!   5
Rule thou in peace, our father, and our lord!
Midſt the remembrance of thy favours paſt,
The meaneſt peaſants moſt admire the laſt. *
May *George*, belov'd by all the nations round,
Live with heav'ns choiceſt conſtant bleſſings
        crown'd!   10
Great God, direct, and guard him from on high,
And from his head let ev'ry evil fly!
And may each clime with equal gladneſs ſee
A monarch's ſmile can ſet his ſubjects free!

* The Repeal of the Stamp Act.

C   On

On being brought from A F R I C A to
A M E R I C A.

'TWAS mercy brought me from my *Pagan*
   land,
Taught my benighted foul to underftand
That there's a God, that there's a *Saviour* too:
Once I redemption neither fought nor knew
Some view our fable race with fcornful eye,   5
" Their colour is a diabolic die."
Remember, *Chriftians*, *Negros*, black as *Cain*,
May be refin'd, and join th' angelic train,

On

On the Death of the Rev. Dr. SEWELL.
1769.

ERE yet the morn its lovely blushes spread,
  See *Sewell* number'd with the happy dead.
Hail, holy man, arriv'd th' immortal shore,
Though we shall hear thy warning voice no more.
Come, let us all behold with wishful eyes   5
The saint ascending to his native skies;
From hence the prophet wing'd his rapt'rous way
To the blest mansions in eternal day
Then begging for the Spirit of our God,
And panting eager for the same abode,   10
Come, let us all with the same vigour rise,
And take a prospect of the blissful skies ;
While on our minds *Chrift's* image is impreft,
And the dear Saviour glows in ev'ry breaft.
Thrice happy faint ! to find thy heav'n at laft,   15
What compenfation for the evils paft !

Great God, incomprehenfible, unknown
By fenfe, we bow at thine exalted throne.
O, while we beg thine excellence to feel,
Thy facred Spirit to our hearts reveal,   20
And give us of that mercy to partake,
Which thou haft promis'd for the *Saviour's* fake!

" *Sewell* is dead."   Swift-pinion'd *Fame* thus
        cry'd.
" Is *Sewell* dead," my trembling tongue reply'd,
O what a blefling in his flight deny'd!   25
How oft for us the holy prophet pray'd!
How oft to us the Word of Life convey'd!
By duty urg'd my mournful verfe to clofe,
I for his tomb this epitaph compofe.

" Lo, here a man, redeem'd by *Jefus*' blood, 30
" A finner once, but now a faint with God;
" Behold ye rich, ye poor, ye fools, ye wife,
" Nor let his monument your heart furprize;
" 'Twill tell you what this holy man has done,
" Which gives him brighter luftre than the fun.
                        " Liften,

" Liften, ye happy, from your feats above.

" I fpeak fincerely, while I fpeak and love,

" He fought the paths of piety and truth,

" By thefe made happy from his early youth !

" In blooming years that grace divine he felt,   40

" Which refcues finners from the chains of guilt.

" Mourn him, ye indigent, whom he has fed,

" And henceforth feek, like him, for living bread;

" Ev'n *Chrift*, the bread defcending from above,

" And afk an int'reft in his faving love.   45

" Mourn him, ye youth, to whom he oft has told

" God's gracious wonders from the times of old.

" I, too have caufe this mighty lofs to mourn,

" For he my monitor will not return.

" O when fhall we to his bleft ftate arrive?   50

" When the fame graces in our bofoms thrive."

On the Death of the Rev. Mr GEORGE WHITEFIELD. 1770.

HAIL, happy faint, on thine immortal throne,
   Poffeft of glory, life, and blifs unknown,
We hear no more the mufic of thy tongue,
Thy wonted auditories ceafe to throng.
Thy fermons in unequall'd accents flow'd,   5
And ev'ry bofom with devotion glow'd,
Thou didft in ftrains of eloquence refin'd
Inflame the heart, and captivat: the mind.
Unhappy we the fetting fun deplore,
So glorious once, but ah! it fhines no more.   10

   Behold the prophet in his tow'ring flight!
He leaves the earth for heav'n's unmeafur'd
      height,
And worlds unknown receive him from our fight.
There *Whitefield* wings with rapid courfe his way,
And fails to *Zion* through vaft feas of day.   15
Thy pray'rs, great faint, and thine inceffant cries
Have pierc'd the bofom of thy native fkies.

                                          Thou

Thou moon haft feen, and all the ftars of light,
How he has wreſtled with his God by night.
He pray'd that grace in ev'ry heart might dwell, 20
He long'd to fee *America* excel;
He charg'd its youth that ev'ry grace divine
Should with full luftre in their conduct ſhine;
That Saviour, which his foul did firſt receive,
The greateſt gift that ev'n a God can give, 25
He freely offer'd to the num'rous throng,
That on his lips with lift'ning pleafure hung.

" Take him, ye wretched, for your only good,
" Take him ye ftarving finners, for your food;
" Ye thirfty, come to this life-giving ftream, 30
" Ye preachers, take him for your joyful theme;
" Take him my dear *Americans*, he faid,
" Be your complaints on his kind bofom laid:
" Take him, ye *Africans*, he longs for you,
" *Impartial Saviour* is his title due · 35
" Waſh'd in the fountain of redeeming blood,
" You ſhall be fons, and kings, and priefts to God."

Great *Countess*, * we *Americans* revere
Thy name, and mingle in thy grief sincere;
New England deeply feels, the *Orphans* mourn,   40
Their more than father will no more return.

But, though arrested by the hand of death,
Whitefield no more exerts his lab'ring breath,
Yet let us view him in th' eternal skies,
Let ev'ry heart to this bright vision rise,   45
While the tomb safe retains its sacred trust,
Till life divine re-animates his dust.

* The Countess of *Huntingdon,* to whom Mr. *Whitefield*
was Chaplain.

On

On the Death of a young Lady of Five Years of Age.

FROM dark abodes to fair etherial light
   Th' enraptur'd innocent has wing'd her flight;
On the kind bosom of eternal love
She finds unknown beatitude above.
This know, ye parents, nor her loss deplore,   5
She feels the iron hand of pain no more;
The dispensations of unerring grace,
Should turn your sorrows into grateful praise;
Let then no tears for her henceforward flow,
No more distress'd in our dark vale below.   10

Her morning sun, which rose divinely bright,
Was quickly mantled with the gloom of night;
But hear in heav'n's blest bow'rs your *Nancy* fair,
And learn to imitate her language there.
" Thou, Lord, whom I behold with glory crown'd,
" By what sweet name, and in what tuneful sound

D

" Wilt

:O

" Wilt thou be prais'd ? Seraphic pow'rs are faint
" Infinite love and majesty to paint.
" To thee let all their grateful voices raise,
" And faints and angels join their songs of
  " praise."   20

Perfect in blifs she from her heav'nly home
Looks down, and smiling beckons you to come;
Why then, fond parents, why these fruitless groans ?
Restrain your tears, and cease your plaintive moans.
Freed from a world of sin, and snares, and pain, 25
Why would you wish your daughter back again ?
No—bow resign'd.   Let hope your grief control,
And check the rising tumult of the soul.
Calm in the prosperous, and adverse day,
Adore the God who gives and takes away ;   30
Eye him in all, his holy name revere,
Upright your actions, and your hearts sincere,
Till having sail'd through life's tempestuous sea,
And from its rocks, and boist'rous billows free,
Yourselves, safe landed on the blifsful shore,   35
Shall join your happy babe to part no more.

                                        On

On the Death of a young Gentleman.

WHO taught thee conflict with the pow'rs
    of night,
To vanquifh Satan in the fields of fight?
Who ftrung thy feeble arms with might unknown,
How great thy conqueft, and how bright thy
    crown!
War with each princedom, throne, and pow'r
    is o'er,   6
The fcene is ended to return no more.
O could my mufe thy feat on high behold,
How deckt with laurel, how enrich'd with gold!
O could fhe hear what praife thine harp em-
    ploys,
How fweet thine anthems, how divine thy joys! 10
What heav'nly grandeur fhould exalt her ftrain!
What holy raptures in her numbers reign!
To footh the troubles of the mind to peace,
To ftill the tumult of life's toffing feas,

To

To eafe the anguifh of the parents heart,   15
What fhall my fympathizing verfe impart ?
Where is the balm to heal fo deep a wound ?
Where fhall a fov'reign remedy be found ?
Look, gracious Spirit, from thine heav'nly bow'r,
And thy full joys into their bofoms pour,   20
The raging tempeft of their grief control,
And fpread the dawn of glory through the foul,
To eye the path the faint departed trod,
And trace him to the bofom of his God.

· To

To a Lady on the Death of her Hufband

GRIM monarch! fee, depriv'd of vital breath,
  A young phyfician in the duft of death:
Doft thou go on inceffant to deftroy,
Our griefs to double, and lay wafte our joy?
Enough thou never yet waft known to fay,   5
Though millions die, the vaffals of thy fway:
Nor youth, nor fcience, nor the ties of love,
Nor aught on earth thy flinty heart can move.
The friend, the fpoufe from his dire dart to fave,
In vain we afk the fovereign of the grave.   10
Fair mourner, there fee thy lov'd *Leonard* laid,
And o'er him fpread the deep impervious fhade;
Clos'd are his eyes, and heavy fetters keep
His fenfes bound in never-waking fleep,
Till time fhall ceafe, till many a ftarry world   15
Shall fall from heav'n, in dire confufion hurl'd,
Till nature in her final wreck fhall lie,
And her laft groan fhall rend the azure fky:

Not

Not, not till then his active soul shall claim
His body, a divine immortal frame.   20

   But see the softly-stealing tears apace
Pursue each other down the mourner's face;
But cease thy tears, bid ev'ry sigh depart,
And cast the load of anguish from thine heart:
From the cold shell of his great soul arise,   25
And look beyond, thou native of the skies;
There fix thy view, where fleeter than the wind
Thy *Leonard* mounts, and leaves the earth behind.
Thyself prepare to pass the vale of night
To join for ever on the hills of light: 30
To thine embrace his joyful spirit moves
To thee, the partner of his earthly loves;
He welcomes thee to pleasures more refin'd,
And better suited to th' immortal mind.

                                  GOLI.

GOLIATH of GATH.
1 SAM. Chap. XVII.

YE martial pow'rs, and all ye tuneful nine,
   Inspire my song, and aid my high design.
The dreadful scenes and toils of war I write,
The ardent warriors, and the fields of fight:
You best remember, and you best can sing   5
The acts of heroes to the vocal string:
Resume the lays with which your sacred lyre,
Did then the poet and the sage inspire.

Now front to front the armies were display'd,
Here *Israel* rang'd, and there the foes array'd;   10
The hosts on two opposing mountains stood,
Thick as the foliage of the waving wood;
Between them an extensive valley lay,
O'er which the gleaming armour pour'd the day,
When from the camp of the *Philistine* foes,   15
Dreadful to view, a mighty warrior rose;
In the dire deeds of bleeding battle skill'd,
The monster stalks the terror of the field.

From

From *Gath* he fprung, *Goliath* was his name,
Of fierce deportment, and gigantic frame·　20
A brazen helmet on his head was plac'd,
A coat of mail his form terrific grac'd,
The greaves his legs, the targe his fhoulders preft:
Dreadful in arms high-tow'ring o'er the reft
A fpear he proudly wav'd, whofe iron head,　25
Strange to relate, fix hundred fhekels weigh'd;
He ftrode along, and fhook the ample field,
While *Phœbus* blaz'd refulgent on his fhield:
Through *Jacob's* race a chilling horror ran,
When thus the huge, enormous chief began:　30

　" Say, what the caufe that in this proud array
" You fet your battle in the face of day?
" One hero find in all your vaunting train,
" Then fee who lofes, and who wins the plain;
" For he who wins, in triumph may demand　35
" Perpetual fervice from the vanquifh'd land:
" Your armies I defy, your force defpife,
" By far inferior in *Philiftia's* eyes:

　　　　　　　　" Produce

" Produce a man, and let us try the fight,
" Decide the conteft, and the victor's right."   40

Thus challeng'd he · all Ifrael ftood amaz'd,
And ev'ry chief in confternation gaz'd;
But Jeffe's fon in youthful bloom appears,
And warlike courage far beyond his years.:
He left the folds, he left the flow'ry meads,   45
And foft receffes of the fylvan fhades.
Now Ifrael's monarch, and his troops arife,
With peals of fhouts afcending to the fkies;
In Elah's vale the fcene of combat lies.

When the fair morning blufh'd with orient
    red,   50
What David's fire enjoin'd the fon obey'd,
And fwift of foot towards the trench he came,
Where glow'd each bofom with the martial flame.
He leaves his carriage to another's care,
And runs to greet his brethren of the war.   55
While yet they fpake the giant-chief arofe,
Repeats the challenge, and infults his foes:

Struck

Struck with the found, and trembling at the view,
Affrighted *Ifrael* from its poſt withdrew.
" Obſerve ye this tremendous foe, they cry'd, 60
" Who in proud vaunts our armies hath defy'd :
" Whoever lays him proſtrate on the plain,
" Freedom in *Ifrael* for his houſe ſhall gain ;
" And on him wealth unknown the king will pour,
" And give his royal daughter for his dow'r." 65

   Then *Jeſſe's* youngeſt hope : " My brethren
     " ſay,
" What ſhall be done for him who takes away
" Reproach from *Jacob*, who deſtroys the chief,
" And puts a period to his country's grief.
" He vaunts the honours of his arms abroad, 70
" And ſcorns the armies of ⸱the living God."

   Thus ſpoke the youth, th' attentive people ey'd
The wond'rous hero, and again reply'd .
" Such the rewards our monarch will beſtow,
" On him who conquers, and deſtroys his foe." 75

                  Eliab

Eliab heard, and kindled into ire
To hear his shepherd-brother thus inquire,
And thus begun? " What errand brought thee?
  " say
" Who keeps thy flock? or does it go astray?
" I know the base ambition of thine heart,   80
" But back in safety from the field depart."

Eliab thus to *Jesse's* youngest heir,
Express'd his wrath in accents most severe.
When to his brother mildly he reply'd,
" What have I done? or what the cause to
  " chide?"   85

The words were told before the king, who sent
For the young hero to his royal tent:
Before the monarch dauntless he began,
" For this *Philistine* fail no heart of man:
" I'll take the vale, and with the giant fight: 90
" I dread not all his boasts, nor all his might."

          E 2   When

When thus the king " Dar'ft thou a ftripling go,

" And venture combat with fo great a foe?

" Who all his days has been inur'd to fight,

" And made its deeds his ftudy and delight : 95

" Battles and bloodfhed brought the monfter forth,

" And clouds and whirlwinds ufher'd in his birth."

When *David* thus · " I kept the fleecy care,

" And out there rufh'd a lion and a bear,

" A tender lamb the hungry lion took, 100

" And with no other weapon than my crook

" Bold I purfu'd, and chas'd him o'er the field,

" The prey deliver'd, and the felon kill'd :

" As thus the lion and the bear I flew,

" So fhall *Goliath* fall, and all his crew : 105

" The God, who fav'd me from thefe beafts of

" prey,

" By me this monfter in the duft fhall lay."

So *David* fpoke. The wond'ring king reply'd;

" Go thou with heav'n and victory on thy fide.

" This coat of mail, this fword gird on," he

" faid, 110

And plac'd a mighty helmet on his head.

The

The coat, the fword, the helm he laid afide,
Nor chofe to venture with thofe arms untry'd,
Then took his ftaff, and to the neighb'ring
  brook
Inftant he ran, and thence five pebbles took.   115
Mean time defcended to *Philiftia's* fon
A radiant cherub, and he thus begun:
" Goliath, well thou know'ft thou haft defy'd
" Yon Hebrew armies, and their God deny'd:
" Rebellious wretch! audacious worm! for-
   bear,   120
" Nor tempt the vengeance of their God too far:
" Them, who with his omnipotence contend,
" No eye fhall pity, and no arm defend:
" Proud as thou art, in fhort liv'd glory great,
" I come to tell thee thine approaching fate.   125
" Regard my words.   The judge of all the gods,
" Beneath whofe fteps the tow'ring mountain nods,
" Will give thine armies to the favage brood,
" That cut the liquid air, or range the wood.
" Thee too a well-aim'd pebble fhall deftroy, 130
" And thou fhalt perifh by a beardlefs boy:
                            " Such

" Such is the mandate from the realms above,

" And fhould I try the vengeance to remove,

" Myfelf a rebel to my king would prove.

" *Goliath* fay, fhall grace to him be fhown, 135

" Who dares heav'ns monarch, and infults his
" throne?"

" Your words are loft on me," the giant
   cries,

While fear and wrath contended in his eyes,

When thus the meffenger from heav'n replies:

" Provoke no more *Jehovah's* awful hand   140

" To hurl its vengeance on thy guilty land:

" He grafps the thunder, and, he wings the
" ftorm,

" Servants their fov'reign's orders to perform."

The angel fpoke, and turn'd his eyes away,

Adding new radiance to the rifing day.   145

Now *David* comes: the fatal ftones demand

His left, the ftaff engag'd his better hand:

The

The giant mov'd, and from his tow'ring height
Survey'd the ftripling, and difdain'd the fight,
And thus began : " Am I a dog with thee ? 150
" Bring'ft thou no armour, but a ftaff to me ?
" The gods on thee their vollied curfes pour,
" And beafts and birds of prey thy flefh de-
   " vour."

   David undaunted thus, " Thy fpear and fhield
" Shall no protection to thy body yield . 155
" *Jehovah's* name ——no other arm I bear,
" I ask no other in this glorious war.
" To-day the Lord of Hofts to me will give
" Vict'ry, to-day thy doom thou fhalt receive ,
" The fate you threaten fhall your own be-
   " come, 160
" And beafts fhall be your animated tomb,
" That all the earth's inhabitants may know
" That there's a God, who governs all below :
" This great affembly too fhall witnefs ftand,
" That needs nor fword, nor fpear, th' Almighty's
   hand ; 165
                      " The

" The battle his, the conqueſt he beſtows,

" And to our pow'r conſigns our hated foes."

Thus *David* ſpoke , *Goliath* heard and came

To meet the hero in the field of fame.

Ah ! fatal meeting to thy troops and thee,   170

But thou waſt deaf to the divine decree ;

Young *David* meets thee, meets thee not in vain;

'Tis thine to periſh on th' enſanguin'd plain

And now the youth the forceful pebble flung,

Philiſtia trembled as it whizz'd along :   175

In his dread forehead, where the helmet ends,

Juſt o'er the brows the well-aim'd ſtone deſcends,

It pierc'd the ſkull, and ſhatter'd all the brain,

Prone on his face he tumbled to the plain :

Goliath's fall no ſmaller terror yields   180

Than riving thunders in aerial fields :

The ſoul ſtill-ling'red in its lov'd abode,

Till conq'ring *David* o'er the giant ſtrode :

Goliath's ſword then laid its maſter dead,

And from the body hew'd the ghaſtly head ; 185

The

The blood in gushing torrents drench'd the plains,
The soul found passage through the spouting
   veins.

And now aloud th' illustrious victor said,
" Where are your boastings now your cham-
   " pion's dead?"
Scarce had he spoke, when the *Philistines* fled :
But fled in vain, the conqu'ror swift purfu'd :
What scenes of slaughter ! and what seas of blood !
There *Saul* thy thousands grasp'd th' impurpled
   sand
In pangs of death the conquest of thine hand ;
And *David* there were thy ten thousands laid: 195
Thus *Israel's* damsels musically play'd.

Near *Gath* and *Ekron* many an hero lay,
Breath'd out their souls, and curs'd the light of
   day :
Their fury, quench'd by death, no longer burns,
And *David* with *Goliath's* head returns,   200
To *Salem* brought, but in his tent he plac'd
The load of armour which the giant grac'd.

His

His monarch faw him coming from the war,
And thus-demanded of the fon of *Ner.*

" Say, who is this amazing youth ? ' he cry'd, 205
When thus the leader of the hoft reply'd ;

" As lives thy foul I know not whence he fprung,
" So great in prowefs though in years fo young ."

" Inquire whofe fon is he," the fov'reign faid,
" Before whofe conq'ring arm *Phikfia* fied." 210
Before the king behold the ftripling ftand,
Gchath's head depending from his hand :
To him the king : " Say of what martial line
" Art thou, young hero, and what fire was thine ?"
He humbly thus, " the fon of *Jeffe* I :   215
" I came the glories of the field to try.

" Small is my tribe, but valiant in the fight ;
" Small is my city, but thy royal right."

" Then take the promis'd gifts," the monarch
     cry'd,
Conferring riches and the royal bride :   220
" Knit to my foul for ever thou remain
" With me, nor quit my regal roof again."

Thoughts

Thoughts on the WORKS of PROVIDENCE.

ARISE, my foul, on wings enraptur'd, rife
   To praife the monarch of the earth and
      fkies,
Whofe goodnefs and beneficence appear
As round its centre moves the rolling year,
Or when the morning glows with rofy charms,   5
Or the fun flumbers in the ocean's arms.
Of light divine be a rich portion-lent
To guide my foul, and favour my intent:
Celeftial mufe, my arduous flight fuftain,
And raife my mind to a feraphic ftrain!   10

   Ador'd for ever be the God unfeen,
Which round the fun revolves this vaft machine,
Though to his eye its mafs a point appears:
Ador'd the God that whirls furrounding fpheres,
Which firft ordain'd that mighty *Sol* fhould
   reign   15
The peerlefs monarch of th' ethereal train:

Of

Of miles twice forty millions is his height,
And yet his radiance dazzles mortal fight
So far beneath—from him th' extended earth
Vigour derives, and ev'ry flow'ry birth ·   20
Vaft through her orb fhe moves with eafy grace
Around her *Phœbus* in unbounded fpace,
True to her courfe th' impetuous ftorm derides,
Triumphant o'er the winds, and furging tides

Almighty, in thefe wond'rous works of thine, 25
What *Pow'r*, what *Wifdom*, and what *Goodnefs*
    fhine ?
And are thy wonders, Lord, by men explor'd,
And yet creating glory unador'd !

Creation fmiles in various beauty gay,
While day to night, and night fucceeds to day : 30
That *Wifdom*, which attends *Jehovah's* ways,
Shines moft confpicuous in the folar rays
Without them, deftitute of heat and light,
This world would be the reign of endlefs
    night :

In

In their excefs how would our race complain, 35
Abhorring life ! how hate its length'ned chain !
From an aduft what num'rous ills would rife ?
What dire contagion taint the burning fkies ?
What peftilential vapours, fraught with death,
Would rife, and overfpread the lands beneath ? 40

III. I fmiling morn, that from the orient main
Afcending doft adorn the heav'nly plain !
So rich, fo various are thy beauteous dies,
That fpread through all the circuit of the fkies,
That, full of thee, my foul in rapture foars,   45
And thy great God, the caufe of all adores.

O'er beings infinite his love extends,
His *Wifdom* rules them, and his *Pow'r* defends.
When tafks diurnal tire the human frame,
The fpirits faint, and dim the vital flame,   50
Then too that ever active bounty fhines,
Which not infinity of fpace confines.
The fable veil, that *Night* in filence draws,
Conceals effect, but fhews th' *Almighty Caufe*;

Night

Night feals in fleep the wide creation fair,   55
And all is peaceful but the brow of care.
Again, gay *Phœbus*, as the day before,
Wakes ev'ry eye, but what fhall wake no more,
Again the face of nature is renew'd,
Which fill appears harmonious, fair, and good. 60
May grateful ftrains falute the fmiling morn,
Before its beams the eaftern hills adorn!

Shall day to day and night to night confpire
To fhow the goodnefs of the Almighty Sire?
This mental voice fhall man regardlefs hear,   65
And never, never raife the filial pray'r?
To-day, O hearken, nor your folly mourn
For time mifpent, that never will return.

But fee the fons of vegetation rife,
And fpread their leafy banners to the fkies.   70
All-wife Almighty Providence we trace
In trees, and plants, and all the flow'ry race;
As clear as in the nobler frame of man,
All lovely copies of the Maker's plan.

                                                The

The pow'r the same that forms a ray of light, 75
That call'd creation from eternal night.
" Let there be light," he said : from his profound
Old *Chaos* heard, and trembled at the sound :
Swift as the word, inspir'd by pow'r divine,
Behold the light around its maker shine, 80
The first fair product of th' omnific God,
And now through all his works diffus'd abroad.

As reason's pow'rs by day our God disclose,
So we may trace him in the night's repose :
Say what is sleep? and dreams how passing
strange ! 85
When action ceafes, and ideas range
Licentious and unbounded o'er the plains,
Where *Fancy's* queen in giddy triumph reigns.
Hear in soft strains the dreaming lover sigh
To a kind fair, or rave in jealousy ; 90
On pleasure now, and now on vengeance bent,
The lab'ring passions struggle for a vent.
What pow'r, O man ! thy *reason* then restores,
So long suspended in nocturnal hours ?

What

What secret hand returns the mental train,   95
And gives improv'd thine active pow'rs again?
From thee, O man, what gratitude should rise!
And, when from balmy sleep thou op'st thine
    eyes,
Let thy first thoughts be praises to the skies.
How merciful our God who thus imparts,   100
O'erflowing tides of joy to human hearts,
When wants and woes might be our righteous lot,
Our God forgetting, by our God forgot!

    Among the mental pow'rs a question rose,
" What most the image of th' Eternal shows?"
When thus to *Reason* (so let *Fancy* rove)
Her great companion spoke immortal *Love*.

    " Say, mighty pow'r, how long shall strife pre-
      vail,
" And with its murmurs load the whisp'ring
    " gale?
" Refer the cause to *Recollection's* shrine,   110
" Who loud proclaims my origin divine,
                        " The

" The caufe whence heav'n and earth began to be,
" And is not man immortaliz'd by me?
" *Reafon* let this moft caufelefs ftrife fubfide."
Thus *Love* pronounc'd, and *Reafon* thus re-
  ply'd.   115

  " Thy birth, celeftial queen ! 'tis mine to own,
" In thee refplendent is the Godhead fhown ;
" Thy words perfuade, my foul enraptur'd feels
" Refiftlefs beauty which thy fmile reveals."
Ardent fhe fpoke, and, kindling at her
    charms,   120
She clafp'd the blooming goddefs in her arms.

  Infinite *Love* where'er we turn our eyes
Appears : this ev'ry creature's wants fupplies ;
This moft is heard in *Nature's* conftant voice,
This makes the morn, and this the eve re-
    joice ,   125
This bids the foft'ring rains and dews defcend
To nourifh all, to ferve one gen'ral end,

                  G   The

The good of man: yet man ungrateful pays
But little homage, and but little praise.
To him, whose works array'd with mercy
　shine,　　　　　　　　　　　　　　130
What songs should rise, how constant, how di-
　vine!

To a Lady on the Death of Three Relations.

WE trace the pow'r of Death from tomb to
  tomb,
And his are all the ages yet to come.
'Tis his to call the planets from on high,
To blacken *Phœbus*, and diſſolve the ſky;
His too, when all in his dark realms are hurl'd, 5
From its firm baſe to ſhake the ſolid world;
His fatal ſceptre rules the ſpacious whole,
And trembling nature rocks from pole to pole.

Awful he moves, and wide his wings are ſpread:
Behold thy brother number'd with the dead! 10
From bondage freed, the exulting ſpirit flies
Beyond *Olympus*, and theſe ſtarry ſkies.
Loſt in our woe for thee, bleſt ſhade, we mourn
In vain; to earth thou never muſt return.
Thy ſiſters too, fair mourner, feel the dart 15
Of Death, and with freſh torture rend thine heart.

Weep not for them, who wish thine happy mind
To rise with them, and leave the world behind.

As a young plant by hurricanes up torn,   20
So near its parent lies the newly born —
But 'midst the bright ethereal train behold
It shines superior on a throne of gold :
Then, mourner, cease ; let hope thy tears restrain,
Smile on the tomb, and sooth the raging pain. 25
On yon blest regions fix thy longing view,
Mindless of sublunary scenes below ;
Ascend the sacred mount, in thought arise,
And seek substantial, and immortal joys ;
Where hope receives, where faith to vision
    springs,   30
And raptur'd seraphs tune th' immortal strings
To strains extatic.   Thou the chorus join,
And to thy father tune the praise divine.

To

To a Clergyman on the Death of his Lady.

WHERE contemplation finds her facred
  fpring,
Where heav'nly mufic makes the arches ring,
Where virtue reigns unfully'd and divine,
Where wifdom thron'd, and all the graces fhine,
There fits thy fpoufe amidft the radiant throng, 5
While praife eternal warbles from her tongue;
There choirs angelic fhout her welcome round,
With perfect blifs, and peerlefs glory crown'd.

'While thy dear mate, to flefh no more confin'd,
Exults a bleft, an heav'n-afcended mind,   10
Say in thy breaft fhall floods of forrow rife?
Say fhall its torrents overwhelm thine eyes?
Amid the feats of heav'n a place is free,
And angels ope their bright ranks for thee;
For thee they wait, and with expectant eye   15
Thy fpoufe leans downward from th' empyreal
  fky:
                                        " O come

" O come away, her longing fpirit cries,

" And fhare with me the raptures of the fkies.

" Our blifs divine to mortals is unknown;

" Immortal life and glory are our own.   20

" There too may the dear pledges of our love

" Arrive, and tafte with us the joys above;

" Attune the harp to more than mortal lays,

" And join with us the tribute of their praife -

" To him, who dy'd ftern juftice to atone,   25

" And make eternal glory all our own.

" He in his death flew ours, and, as he rofe,

" He crufh'd the dire dominion of our foes;

" Vain were their hopes to put the God to flight,

" Chain us to hell, and bar the gates of light." 30

She fpoke, and turn'd from mortal fcenes her eyes,

Which beam'd celeftial radiance o'er the fkies.

Then thou, dear man, no more with grief re-
    tire,

Let grief no longer damp devotion's fire,

But rife fublime, to equal blifs afpire.   35

Thy

Thy fighs no more be wafted by the wind,
No more complain, but be to heav'n-refign'd.
'Twas thine t' unfold the oracles divine,
To footh our woes the tafk was alfo thine;
Now forrow is incumbent on thy heart,   40
'Permit the mufe a cordial to impart,
Who can to thee their tend'reft aid refufe?
To dry thy tears how longs the heav'nly mufe!

An H Y M N to the Morning.

ATTEND my lays, ye ever honour'd nine,
 Assist my labours, and my strains refine;
In smoothest numbers pour the notes along,
For bright *Aurora* now demands my song.

Aurora hail, and all the thousands dies,   5
Which deck thy progress through the vaulted
 skies :
The morn awakes, and wide extends her rays,
On ev'ry leaf the gentle zephyr plays;
Harmonious lays the feather'd race resume,
Dart the bright eye, and shake the painted
 plume.   10

 Ye shady groves, your verdant gloom display
To shield your poet from the burning day :
Calliope awake the sacred lyre,
While thy fair sisters fan the pleasing fire:

        The

The bow'rs, the gales, the variegated fkies   15
In all their pleafures in my bofom rife.

See in the eaft th' illuftrious king of day!
His rifing radiance drives the fhades away—
But Oh! I feel his fervid beams too ftrong,
And fcarce begun, concludes th' abortive fong, 20

H   An

An H Y M N to the EVENING.

SOON as the fun forfook the eaftern main
  The pealing thunder fhook the heav'nly
    plain;
Majeftic grandeur! From the zephyr's wing,
Exhales the incenfe of the blooming fpring
Soft purl the ftreams, the birds renew their
    notes,   5
And through the air their mingled mufic floats.

  Through all the heav'ns what beauteous dies are
    fpread!
But the weft glories in the deepeft red
So may our breafts with ev'ry virtue glow,
The living temples of our God below!   10

  Fill'd with the praife of him who gives the
    light,
And draws the fable curtains of the night,

                        Let

Let placid flumbers footh each weary mind,
At morn to wake more heav'nly, more refin'd ;
So fhall the labours of the day begin   15
More pure, more guarded from the fnares of fin.

Night's leaden fceptre feals my drowfy eyes,
Then ceafe, my fong, till fair *Aurora* rife.

Isaiah lxiii. 1—8.

SAY, heav'nly mufe, what king, or mighty
   God,
That moves fublime from *Idumea's* road?
In *Bozrch's* dies, with martial glories join'd,
His purple vefture waves upon the wind.
Why thus enrob'd delights he to appear   5
In the dread image of the *Pow'r* of war?

Comprefs'd in wrath the fwelling wine-prefs
   groan'd,
It bled, and pour'd the gufhing purple round

" Mine was the act," th' Almighty Saviour
   faid,
And fhook the dazzling glories of his head,   10
" When all forfook I trod the prefs alone,
" And conquer'd by omnipotence my own ;
" For man's releafe fuftain'd the pond'rous load,
" For man the wrath of an immortal God ·
                   " To

" To execute th' Eternal's dread command   15
" My foul I facrific'd with willing hand,
" Sinlefs I ftood before the avenging frown,
" Atoning thus for vices not my own."

His eye the ample field of battle round
Survey'd, but no created fuccours found;   20
His own omnipotence fuftain'd the fight,
His vengeance funk the haughty foes in night;
Beneath his feet the proftrate troops were fpread,
And round him lay the dying, and the dead.

Great God, what light'ning flafhes from thine
     eyes ?   25
What pow'r withftands if thou indignant rife ?

Againft thy *Zion* though her foes may rage,
And all their cunning, all their ftrength engage,
Yet fhe ferenely on thy bofom lies,
Smiles at their arts, and all their force defies.   30

On Recollection.

MNEME begin. Infpire, ye facred nine,
Your vent'rous *Afric* in her great defign.
Mneme, immortal pow'r, I trace thy fpring:
Affift my ftrains, while I thy glories fing:
The acts of long departed years, by thee   5
Recover'd, in due order rang'd we fee .
Thy pow'r the long-forgotten calls from night,
That fweetly plays before the *fancy's* fight.

   Mneme in our nocturnal vifions pours
The ample treafure of her fecret ftores;   10
Swift from above fhe wings her filent flight
Through *Phœbe's* realms, fair regent of the
      night,
And, in her pomp of images difplay'd,
To the high-raptur'd poet gives her aid,
Through the unbounded regions of the mind, 15
Diffufing light celeftial and refin'd.

                                        The

The heav'nly *phantom* paints the actions done
By ev'ry tribe beneath the rolling sun.

Mneme, enthron'd within the human breast,
Has vice condemn'd, and ev'ry virtue blest.   20
How sweet the sound when we her plaudit hear ?
Sweeter than music to the ravish'd ear,
Sweeter than *Maro's* entertaining strains
Resounding through the groves, and hills, and
    plains.
But how is *Mneme* dreaded by the race,   25
Who scorn her warnings, and despise her grace ?
By her unveil'd each horrid crime appears,
Her awful hand a cup of wormwood bears.
Days, years mispent, O what a hell of woe !
Hers the worst tortures that our souls can know.   30

Now eighteen years their destin'd course have
    run,
In fast succession round the central sun.
How did the follies of that period pass
Unnotic'd, but behold them writ in brass !

In

In Recollection fee them frefh return,   35
And fure 'tis mine to be afham'd, and mourn.

O *Virtue*, fmiling in immortal green,,
Do thou exert thy pow'r, and change the fcene;
Be thine employ to guide my future days,
And mine to pay the tribute of my praife.   40

Of *Recollection* fuch the pow'r enthron'd
In ev'ry breaft, and thus her pow'r is own'd.
·The wretch, who dar'd the vengeance of the fkies,
At laft awakes in horror and furprize,
By her alarm'd, he fees impending fate,   45
He howls in anguifh, and repents too late.
But O! what peace, what joys are hers t' impart
To ev'ry holy, ev'ry upright heart!
'Thrice bleft the man, who, in her facred fhrine,
Feels himfelf fhelter'd from the wrath divine! 50

* On IMAGINATION,

THY various works, imperial queen, we fee,
    How bright their forms! how deck'd with
        pomp by thee!
Thy wond'rous acts in beauteous order ftand,
And all atteft how potent is thine hand.

From *Helicon's* refulgent heights attend,   5
Ye facred choir, and my attempts befriend:
To tell her glories with a faithful tongue,
Ye blooming graces, triumph in my fong.

Now here, now there, the roving *Fancy* flies,
Till fome lov'd object ftrikes her wand'ring
    eyes,   10
Whofe filken fetters all the fenfes bind,
And foft captivity involves the mind.

I   *Imagi-*

Imagination ! who can fing thy force?
Or who defcribe the fwiftnefs of thy courfe?
Soaring through air to find the bright abode,   15
Th' empyreal palace of the thund'ring God,
We on thy pinions can furpafs the wind,
And leave the rolling univerfe behind :
From ftar to ftar the mental optics rove,
Meafure   the   fkies,   and   range   the   realms
     above.   20
There in one view we grafp the mighty whole,
Or with new worlds amaze th' unbounded foul.

  Though *Winter* frowns to *Fancy's* raptur'd
     eyes
The fields may flourifh, and gay fcenes arife;
The frozen deeps may break their iron bands, 25
And bid their waters murmur o'er the fands.
Fair *Flora* may refume her fragrant reign,
And with her flow'ry riches deck the plain;
Sylvanus may diffufe his honours round,
And all the foreft may with leaves be crown'd : 30
                                        Show'rs

Show'rs may defcend, and dews their gems dif-
    clofe,

And nectar fparkle on the blooming rofe.

Such is thy pow'r, nor are thine orders vain,

O thou the leader of the mental train ·

In full perfection all thy works are wrought,   35

And thine the fceptre o'er the realms of thought.

Before thy throne the fubject-paffions bow,

'Of fubject-paffions fov'reign ruler Thou;

At thy command joy rufhes on the heart,

And through the glowing veins the fpirits dart. 40

- Fancy might now her filken pinions try

To rife from earth, and fweep th' expanfe on
    high;

From Tithon's bed now might Aurora rife,

Her cheeks all glowing with celeftial dies,

While a pure ftream of light o'erflows the
    fkies,   45

The monarch of the day I might behold,

And all the mountains tipt with radiant gold,

              But

But I reluctant leave the pleasing views,
Which *Fancy* dresses to delight the *Muse*,
Winter austere forbids me to aspire,   50
And northern tempests damp the rising fire,
They chill the tides of *Fancy s* flowing sea,
Cease then, my song, cease the unequal lay.

A Fu.

A Funeral P O E M on the Death of C. E.
an Infant of Twelve Months.

THROUGH airy roads he wings his inftant
    flight
To purer regions of celeftial light;
Enlarg'd he fees unnumber'd fyftems roll,
Beneath him fees the univerfal whole,
Planets on planets run their deftin'd round,   5
And circling wonders fill the vaft profound.
Th' ethereal now, and now th' empyreal fkies
With growing fplendors ftrike his wond'ring eyes:
The angels view him with delight unknown,
Prefs his foft hand, and feat him on his throne;
Then fmiling thus. " To this divine abode,
" The feat of faints, of feraphs, and of God,
" Thrice welcome thou." The raptur'd babe
    replies,
" Thanks to my God, who fnatch'd me to the
    " fkies,

                      " E'er

" E'er vice triumphant had poffefs'd my heart, 15
" E'er yet the tempter had beguil'd my heart,
" E'er yet on fin's bafe actions I was bent,
" E'er yet I knew temptation's dire intent ;
" E'er yet the lafh for horrid crimes I felt,
" E'er vanity had led my way to guilt,   20
" But, foon arriv'd at my celeftial goal,
" Full glories rufh on my expanding foul."
Joyful he fpoke : exulting cherubs round
Clapt their glad wings, the heav'nly vaults refound.

Say, parents, why this unavailing moan ?   25
Why heave your penfive bofoms with the groan ?
To *Charles*, the happy fubject of my fong,
A brighter world, and nobler ftrains belong.
Say would you tear him from the realms above
By thoughtlefs wifhes, and prepoft'rous love ? 30
Doth his felicity increafe your pain ?
Or could you welcome to this world again
The heir of blifs ? with a fuperior air
Methinks he anfwers with a fmile fevere,
" Thrones and dominions cannot tempt me
    " there."
                                                            35

                                                        But

But ftill you cry, " Can we the figh forbear,
" And ftill and ftill muft we not pour the tear?
" Our only hope, more dear than vital breath,
" Twelve moons revolv'd, becomes the prey of
   " death;
" Delightful infant, nightly vifions give   40
" Thee to our arms, and we with joy receive,
" We fain would clafp the *Phantom* to our breaft,
" The *Phantom* flies, and leaves the foul unbleft."

To yon bright regions let your faith afcend,
Prepare to join your deareft infant friend
In pleafures without meafure, without end.

To Captain H——D, of the 65th Regiment.

SAY, muſe divine, can hoſtile ſcenes delight
   The warrior's boſom in the fields of fight?
Lo! here the chriſtian, and the hero join
With mutual grace to form the man divine.
In H——D ſee with pleaſure and ſurprize,   5
Where *valour* kindles, and where *virtue* lies
Go, hero brave, ſtill grace the poſt of fame,
And add new glories to thine honour'd name,
Still to the field, and ſtill to virtue true ·
Britannia glories in no ſon like you.   10

To the Right Honourable WILLIAM, Earl
of DARTMOUTH, His Majesty's Principal Secre-
tary of State for North America, &c.

HA I L, happy day, when, fmiling like the
    morn,
Fair *Freedom* rofe *New-England* to adorn:
The northern clime beneath her genial ray,
Dartmouth, congratulates thy blifsful fway:
Elate with hope her race no longer mourns;   5
Each foul expands, each grateful bofom burns,
While in thine hand with pleafure we behold
The filken reins, and *Freedom's* charms unfold.
Long loft to realms beneath the northern fkies,
She fhines fupreme, while hated *faction* dies: 10
Soon as appear'd the *Goddefs* long defir'd,
Sick at the view, fhe languifh'd and expir'd;
Thus from the fplendors of the morning light
The owl in fadnefs feeks the caves of night.

K

No

No more, *America*, in mournful ftrain   15
Of wrongs, and grievance unredrefs'd complain,
No longer fhall thou dread the iron chain,
Which wanton *Tyranny* with lawlefs hand
Had made, and with it meant t' enflave the land.

Should you, my lord, while you perufe my
    fong,   20
Wonder from whence my love of *Freedom* fprung,
Whence flow thefe wifhes for the common good,
By feeling hearts alone beft underftood,
I, young in life, by feeming cruel fate
Was fnatch'd from *Afric's* fancy'd happy feat: 25
What pangs excruciating muft moleft,
What forrows labour in my parent's breaft?
Steel'd was that foul and by no mifery mov'd
That from a father feiz'd his babe belov'd:
Such, fuch my cafe.   And can I then but
    pray   30
Others may never feel tyrannic fway?

For

For favours paft, great Sir, our thanks are due,
And thee we afk thy favours to renew,
Since in thy pow'r, as in thy will before,
To footh the griefs, which thou did'ft once de-
       plore.   35
May heav'nly grace the facred fanction give
To all thy works, and thou for ever live
Not only on the wings of fleeting *Fame*,
Though praife immortal crowns the patriot's
       name,
But to conduct to heav'ns refulgent fane,   40
May fiery courfers fweep th' ethereal plain,
And bear thee upwards to that bleft abode,
Where, like the prophet, thou fhalt find thy God.

K 2   ODE

O D E to N E P T U N E.

On Mrs W—'s Voyage to England

I.

WHILE raging tempests shake the shore,
  While Æ'lus' thunders round us roar,
And sweep impetuous o'er the plain
Be still, O tyrant of the main,
Nor let thy brow cortracted frowns betray,   5
While my *Susannah* skims the wat'ry way.

II.

The *Pow'r* propitious hears the lay,
The blue ey'd daughters of the sea
With sweeter cadence glide along,
And *Thames* responsive joins the song.   10
Pleas'd with their notes *Sol* sheds benign his ray,
And double radiance decks the face of day.

III. To

III

To court thee to *Britannia*'s arms
  Serene the climes and mild the sky,
Her region boasts unnumber'd charms,   15
  Thy welcome smiles in ev'ry eye
Thy promise, *Neptune* keep, record my pray'r,
Nor give my wishes to the empty air.

Boston, October 10, 1772.

To

To a Lady on her coming to North-America
with her Son, for the Recovery of her Health.

INdulgent muse! my grov'ling mind inspire,
  And fill my bosom with celestial fire.

See from *Jamaica's* fervid shore she moves,
Like the fair mother of the blooming loves,
When from above the *Goddess* with her hand   5
Fans the soft breeze, and lights upon the land;
Thus she on *Neptune's* wat'ry realm reclin'd
Appear'd, and thus invites the ling'ring wind.

" Arise, ye winds, *America* explore,
" Waft me, ye gales, from this malignant
   " shore;   10
" The *Northern* milder climes I long to greet,
" There hope that health will my arrival meet."
Soon as she spoke in my ideal view
The winds assented, and the vessel flew.

                              Madam,

Madam, your fpoufe bereft of wife and fon, 15
In the grove's dark receffes pours his moan ;
Each branch, wide-fpreading to the ambient fky,
Forgets its verdure, and fubmits to die.

From thence I turn, and leave the fultry plain,
And fwift purfue thy paffage o'er the main : 20
The fhip arrives before the fav'ring wind,
And makes the *Philadelphian* port affign'd,
Thence I attend you to *Boftonia's* arms,
Where gen'rous friendfhip ev'ry bofom warms :
Thrice welcome here ! may health revive again, 25
Bloom on thy cheek, and bound in ev'ry vein !
Then back return to gladden ev'ry heart,
And give your fpoufe his foul's far dearer part,
Receiv'd again with what a fweet furprize,
The tear in tranfport ftarting from his eyes ! 30
While his attendant fon with b'ooming grace
Springs to his father's ever dear embrace.
With fhouts of joy *Jamaica's* rocks refound,
With fhouts of joy the country rings around.

To

To a LADY on her remarkable Prefervation
in an Hurricane in *North-Carolina.*

THOUGH thou did'ft hear the tempeft from
        afar,
And felt'ft the horrors of the wat'ry war,
To me unknown, yet on this peaceful fhore
Methinks I hear the ftorm tumultuous roar,
And how ftern *Boreas* with impetuous hand   5
Compell'd the *Nereids* to ufurp the land.
Reluctant rofe the daughters of the main,
And flow afcending glided o'er the plain,
Till *Æc'us* in his rapid chariot drove
In gloomy grandeur from the vault above   10
Furious he comes.   His winged fons obey
Their frantic fire, and madden all the fea.
The billows rave, the wind's fierce tyrant roars,
And with his thund'ring terrors fhakes the fhores:
Broken by waves the veffel's frame is rent,   15
And ftrows with planks the wat'ry element.

                                            But

But thee, *Maria*, a kind *Nereid's* fhield
Preferv'd from finking, and thy form upheld :
And fure fome heav'nly oracle defign'd
At that dread crifis to inftruct thy mind   20
Things of eternal confequence to weigh,
And to thine heart juft feelings to convey
Of things above, and of the future doom,
And what the births of the dread world to come.

From tofling feas I welcome thee to land.   25
" Refign her, *Nereid*," 'twas thy God's command.
Thy fpoufe late buried, as thy fears conceiv'd,
Again returns, thy fears are all reliev'd :
Thy daughter blooming with fuperior grace
Again thou fee'ft, again thine arms embrace ; 30
O come, and joyful fhow thy fpoufe his heir,
And what the bleflings of maternal care !

To a LADY and her Children, on the Death of her Son and their Brother.

O'Erwhelming forrow now demands my fong:
From death the overwhelming forrow fprung.
What flowing tears ? What hearts with grief op-
preft ?
What fighs on fighs heave the fond parent's
breaft ?
The brother weeps, the haplefs fifters join   5
Th' increafing woe, and fwell the cryftal brine ;
The poor, who once his gen'rous bounty fed,
Droop, and bewail their benefactor dead.
In death the friend, the kind companion lies,
And in one death what various comfort dies !   10

Th' unhappy mother fees the fanguine rill
Forget to flow, and nature's wheels ftand ftill,
But fee from earth his fpirit far remov'd,
And know no grief recals your beft-belov'd :

He,

He, upon pinions fwifter than the wind,   15
Has left mortality's fad fcenes behind
For joys to this terreftrial ftate unknown,
And glories richer than the monarch's crown.
Of virtue's fteady courfe the prize behold !
What bl.fsful wonders to his mind unfold !   20
But of celeftial joys I fing in vain:
Attempt not, mufe, the too advent'rous ftrain.

    No more in briny fhow'rs, ye friends around,
Or bathe his clay, or wafte them on the ground:
Still do you weep, ftill wifh for his return ?   25
How cruel thus to wifh, and thus to mourn ?
No more for him the ftreams of forrow pour,
But hafte to join him on the heav'nly fhore,
On harps of gold to tune immortal lays,
And to your God immortal anthems raife.   30

L 2   To

To a Gentleman and Lady on the Death of
the Lady's Brother and Sister, and a Child
of the Name *Avis*, aged one Year.

ON *Death's* domain intent I fix my eyes,
Where human nature in vaft ruin lies.
With penfive mind I fearch the drear abode,
Where the great conqu'ror has his fpoils beftow'd;
There there the off-pring of fix thoufand years   5
In endlefs numbers to my view appears
Whole kingdoms in his gloomy den are thruft,
And nations mix with their primeval duft:
Infatiate ftill he gluts the ample tomb,
His is the prefent, his the age to come.   10
See here a brother, here a fifter fpread,
And a fweet daughter mingled with the dead.

But, *Madam*, let your grief be laid afide,
And let the fountain of your tears be dry'd,
In vain they flow to wet the dufty plain,   15
Your fighs are wafted to the fkies in vain,

Your

Your pains they witnefs, but they can no more,
While *Death* reigns tyrant o'er this mortal-fhore.

The glowing ftars and filver queen of light
At laft muft perifh in the gloom of night :   20
Refign thy friends to that Almighty hand,
Which gave them life, and bow to his command ;
Thine *Avis* give without a murm'ring heart,
Though half thy foul be fated to depart.
To fhining guards confign thine infant care   25
To waft triumphant through the feas of air :
Her foul enlarg'd to heav'nly pleafure fprings,
She feeds on truth and uncreated things.
Methinks I hear her in the realms above,
And leaning forward with a filial love,   30
Invite you there to fhare immortal blifs
Unknown, untafted in a ftate like this.
With tow'ring hopes, and glowing grace arife,
And feek beatitude beyond the fkies.

On the Death of Dr. SAMUEL MARSHALL.
1771.

THROUGH thickeſt glooms look back,
    immortal ſhade,
On that confuſion which thy death has made;
Or from *Olympus'* height look down, and ſee
A *Town* involv'd in grief bereft of thee.
Thy *Lucy* ſees thee mingle with the dead,   5
And rends the graceful treſſes from her head,
Wild in her woe, with grief unknown oppreſt
Sigh follows ſigh deep heaving from her breaſt.

Too quickly fled, ah! whither art thou gone?
Ah! loſt for ever to thy wife and ſon!   10
The hapleſs child, thine only hope and heir,
Clings round his mother's neck, and weeps his
    ſorrows there.
The loſs of thee on *Tyler's* ſoul returns,
And *Boſton* for her dear phyſician mourns.

When

When ſickneſs call'd for *Marſhall's* healing
    hand, 15
With what compaſſion did his ſoul expand?
In him we found the father and the friend:
In life how lov'd! how honour'd in his end!

And muſt not then our *Æſculapius* ſtay
To bring his ling'ring infant into day? 20
The babe unborn in the dark womb is toſt,
And ſeems in anguiſh for its father loſt.

Gone is *Apollo* from his houſe of earth,
But leaves the ſweet memorials of his worth:
The common parent, whom we all deplore, 25
From yonder world unſeen muſt come no more,
Yet 'midſt our woes immortal hopes attend
The ſpouſe, the ſire, the univerſal friend.

To

To a GENTLEMAN on his Voyage to *Great-Britain*
for the Recovery of his Health.

WHILE others chant of gay *Elysian* scenes,
   Of balmy zephyrs, and of flow'ry plains,
My song more happy speaks a greater name,
Feels higher motives and a nobler flame.
For thee, O R——, the muse attunes her strings, 5
And mounts sublime above inferior things.

  I sing not now of green embow'ring woods,
I sing not now the daughters of the floods,
I sing not of the storms o'er ocean driv'n,
And how they howl'd along the waste of heav'n, 10
But I to R—— would paint the *British* shore,
And vast *Atlantic*, not untry'd before :
Thy life impair'd commands thee to arise,
Leave these bleak regions, and inclement skies,
Where chilling winds return the winter past,   15
And nature shudders at the furious blast.

                          O thou

O thou ftupendous, earth-enclofing main
Exert thy wonders to the world again!
If ere thy pow'r prolong'd the fleeting breath,
Turn'd back the fhafts, and mock'd the gates of
    death, 20
If ere thine air difpens'd an healing pow'r,
Or fnatch'd the victim from the fatal hour,
This equal cafe demands thine equal care,
And equal wonders may this patient fhare.
But unavailing, frantic is the dream 25
To hope thine aid without the aid of him
Who gave thee birth, and taught thee where to
    flow,
And in thy waves his various bleffings fhow.

May R— return to view his native fhore
Replete with vigour not his own before, 30
Then fhall we fee with pleafure and furprize,
And own thy work, great Ruler of the fkies!

        M   To

To the Rev. DR. THOMAS AMORY
on reading his Sermons on DAILY DEVOTION,
in which that Duty is recommended and assisted.

TO cultivate in ev'ry noble mind
   Habitual grace, and sentiments refin'd,
Thus while you strive to mend the human heart,
Thus while the heav'nly precepts you impart,
O may each bosom catch the sacred fire,   5
And youthful minds to *Virtue's* throne aspire !

When God's eternal ways you set in sight,
And *Virtue* shines in all her native light,
In vain would *Vice* her works in night conceal,
For *Wisdom's* eye pervades the sable veil.   10

Artists may paint the sun's effulgent rays,
But *Amory's* pen the brighter God displays :
While his great works in *Amory's* pages shine,
And while he proves his essence all divine,

                        The

The Atheift fure no more can boaft aloud   15
Of chance, or nature, and exclude the God;
As if the clay without the potter's aid
Should rife in various forms, and fhapes felf-made,
Or worlds above with orb o'er orb profound
Self-mov'd could run the everlafting round.   20
It cannot be — unerring *Wifdom* guides
With eye propitious, and o'er all prefides.

Still profper, *Amory !* ftill may'ft thou receive
The warmeft bleffings which a mufe can give,
And when this tranfitory ftate is o'er,   25
When kingdoms fall, and fleeting *Fame's* no more,
May *Amory* triumph in immortal fame,
A nobler title, and fuperior name !

On

On the Death of J. C an Infant.

NO more the flow'ry scenes of pleasure rise,
   Nor charming prospects greet the mental
    eyes,
No more with joy we v ew that lovely face
Smiling, disportive, flush'd with ev'ry grace.

  The tear of sorrow flows from ev'ry eye,   5
Groans answer groans, and sighs to sighs reply ,
What sudden pangs shot thro' each ach'ng heart,
When, *Death*, thy messenger dispatch'd his dart ?
Thy dread attendants, all-destroying *Pow'r*,
Hurried the infant to his mortal hour.   10
Could'ft thou unpitying close thofe radiant
    eyes ?
Or fail'd his artless beauties to surprize ?
Could not his innocence thy stroke controul,
Thy purpose shake, and soften all thy soul ?

                      The

The blooming babe, with fhades of *Death* o'er-
    fpread,   15
No more fhall fmile, no more fhall raife its
    head,
But, like a branch that from the tree is torn,
Falls proftrate, wither'd, languid, and forlorn.
" Where flies my *James* ?" 'tis thus I feem to
    hear
The parent afk, " Some angel tell me where 20
" He wings his paffage thro' the yielding air ?"
Methinks a cherub bending from the fkies
Obferves the queftion, and ferene replies,
" In heav'ns high palaces your babe appears :
" Prepare to meet him, and difmifs your tears " 25
Shall not th' intelligence your grief reftrain,
And turn the mournful to the chearful ftrain ?
Ceafe your complaints, fufpend each rifing figh,
Ceafe to accufe the Ruler of the fky.
Parents, no more indulge the falling tear :   30
Let *Faith* to heav'n's refulgent domes repair,
There fee your infant, like a feraph glow .
What charms celeftial in his numbers flow

                        Melodious,

Melodious, while the foul-enchanting ftrain
Dwells on his tongue, and fills th'ethereal plain? 35
Enough—for ever ceafe your murm'ring breath,
Not as a foe, but friend converfe with *Death*,
Since to the port of happinefs unknown
He brought that treafure which you call your own.
The gift of heav'n intrufted to your hand   40
Chearful refign at the divine command :
Not at your bar muft fov'reign *Wifdom* ftand.

An H Y M N to HUMANITY.
To S. P. G. Efq;

I.

LO ! for this dark terreftrial ball
Forfakes his azure-paved hall
    A prince of heav'nly birth !
Divine *Humanity* behold.
What wonders rife, what charms unfold   5
    At his defcent to earth !

II.

The bofoms of the great and good
With wonder and delight he view'd,
    And fix'd his empire there :
Him, clofe compreffing to his breaft,   10
The fire of gods and men addrefs'd,
    " My fon, my heav'nly fair !

III. " Defcend

III.

" Defcend to earth, there place thy throne;
" To fuccour man's afflicted fon
    " Each human heart infpire   15
" To act in bounties unconfin'd
" Enlarge the clofe contracted mind,
    " And fill it with thy fire "

IV.

Quick as the word, with fwift career
He wings his courfe from ftar to ftar,   20
    And leaves the bright abode.
The *Virtue* did his charms impart;
Their G——y ¹ then thy raptur'd heart
    Perceiv'd the rufhing God:

V.

For when thy pitying eye did fee   25
The languid mufe in low degree,
    Then, then at thy defire
Defcended the celeflial nine;
O'er me methought they deign'd to fhine,
    And deign'd to ftring my lyre.   30

VI. Can

VI.

Can *Afric's* mufe forgetful prove?
Or can fuch friendfhip fail to move
    A tender human heart?
Immortal *Friendfhip* laurel-crown'd
The fmiling *Graces* all furround   35
    With ev'ry heav'nly *Art.*

To the Honourable T. H. Efq; on the Death
of his Daughter.

WHILE deep you mourn beneath the
cyprefs-fhade
The hand of Death, and your dear daughter laid
In duft, whofe abfence gives your tears to flow,
And racks your bofom with inceffant woe,
Let *Recollection* take a tender part,   5
Affuage the raging tortures of your heart,
Still the wild tempeft of tumultuous grief,
And pour the heav'nly nectar of relief:
Sufpend the figh, dear Sir, and check the groan,
Divinely bright your daughter's *Virtues* fhone: 10
How free from fcornful pride her gentle mind,
Which ne'er its aid to indigence declin'd!
Expanding free, it fought the means to prove
Unfailing charity, unbounded love!

She unreluctant flies to fee no more   15
Her dear-lov'd parents on earth's dufky fhore:

Impatient

Impatient heav'n's refplendent goal to gain,
She with fwift progrefs cuts the azure plain,
Where grief fubfides, where changes are no more,
And life's tumultuous billows ceafe to roar; 20
She leaves her earthly manfion for the fkies,
Where new creations feaft her wond'ring eyes.

To heav'n's high mandate chearfully refign'd
She mounts, and leaves the rolling globe behind;
She, who late wifh'd that *Leonard* might return, 25
Has ceas'd to languifh, and forgot to mourn;
To the fame high empyreal manfions come,
She joins her fpoufe, and fmiles upon the tomb:
And thus I hear her from the realms above:
" Lo! this the kingdom of celeftial love! 30
" Could ye, fond parents, fee our prefent blifs,
" How foon would you each figh, each fear dif-
    " mifs?
" Amidft unutter'd pleafures whilft I play
" In the fair funfhine of celeftial day,
" As far as grief affects an happy foul 35
" So far doth grief my better mind controul,

" To

" To fee on earth my aged parents mourn,

" And fecret wifh for T——l to return ·

" Let brighter fcenes your ev'ning-hours em-
 " ploy ·

" Converfe with heav'n, and tafte the promis'd
 " joy."   40

NIOBE

NIOBE in Diftrefs for her Children flain by
   APOLLO, from *Ovid's* Metamorphofes, Book VI.
   and from a view of the Painting of Mr. *Richard*
   Wilfon

APOLLO's wrath to man the dreadful
         fpring
Of ills innum'rous, tuneful goddefs, fing!
Thou who did'ft firft th' ideal pencil give,
And taught'ft the painter in his works to live,
Infpire with glowing energy of thought,   5
What *Wilfon* painted, and what *Ovid* wrote.
Mufe! lend thy aid, nor let me fue in vain,
Tho' laft and meaneft of the rhyming train!
O guide my pen in lofty ftrains to fhow
The *Phrygian* queen, all beautiful in woe.   10

   'Twas where *Mæonia* fpreads her wide domain
Niobe dwelt, and held her potent reign:
See in her hand the regal fceptre fhine,
The wealthy heir of *Tantalus* divine,

                                           He

He moft diftinguifh'd by *Dodonean Jove*,   15
To approach the tables of the gods above:
Her grandfire *Atlas*, who with mighty pains
Th' ethereal axis on his neck fuftains ·
Her other gran fire on the throne on h gh
Rolls the loud-pealing thunder thro' the fky   20

Her fpoufe, *Amphion*, who from Jove too fprings,
Divinely taught to fweep the founding ftrings

Seven fprightly fons the royal bed adorn,
Seven daughters beauteous as the op'ning morn,
As when *Aurora* fills the ravifh'd fight,   25
And decks the orient realms with rofy light
From their bright eyes the living fplendors play,
Nor can beholders bear the flafhing ray

Wherever, *Niobe*, thou turn'ft th ne eyes,
New beauties kindle, and new joys arife !   30
But thou had'ft far the happier mother prov'd,
If this fair offspring had been lefs belov'd:

                                        What

What if their charms exceed *Aurora's* teint,
No words could tell them, and no pencil paint,
Thy love too vehement haftens to deftroy   35
Each blooming maid, and each celeftial boy.

Now *Manto* comes, endu'd with mighty fkill,
The paft to explore, the future to reveal.
Thro' *Thebes'* wide ftreets *Tirefia's* daughter came,
Divine *Latona's* mandate to proclaim: 40
The Theban maids to hear the orders ran,
When thus *Mæonia's* prophetefs began:

" Go, *Thebans!* great *Latona's* will obey,
" And pious tribute at her altars pay :
" With rights divine, the goddefs be implor'd, 45
" Nor be her facred offspring unador'd."
Thus *Manto* fpoke.   The *Theban* maids obey,
And pious tribute to the goddefs pay.
The rich perfumes afcend in waving fpires,
And altars blaze with confecrated fires;   50
The fair affembly moves with graceful air,
And leaves of laurel bind the flowing hair.

Niobe

Niobe comes with all her royal race,
With charms unnumber'd, and superior grace :
Her *Phrygian* garments of delightful hue,   55
Inwove with gold, refulgent to the v ew,
Beyond description beautiful she moves
L ke heav'nly *Venus*, 'midst her smiles and loves .
She views around the supplicating train,
And shakes her graceful head with stern dif-
    dain,   60
Proudly she turns around her lofty eyes,
And thus reviles celestial deities
" What madness drives the *Theban* ladies fair
" To give their incense to surrounding air ?
" Say why this new sprung deity preferr'd ?   65
" Why vainly fancy your petitions heard ?
" Or say why *Cœus*' offspring is obey'd,
" While to my goddeship no tribute's paid ?
" For me no altars blaze with living fires,
" No bullock bleeds, no frankincense transpires, 70
" Tho' *Cadmus*' palace, not unknown to fame,
" And *Phrygian* nations all revere my name.
                          " Where'er

" Where'er I turn my eyes vaft wealth I find.

" Lo ! here an emprefs with a goddefs join'd.

" What, fhall a *Titanefs* be deify'd,   75

" To whom the fpacious earth a couch deny'd?

" Nor heav'n, nor earth, nor fea receiv'd your

    " queen,

" 'Till pitying *Delos* took the wand'rer in.

" Round me what a large progeny is fpread !

" No frowns of fortune has my foul to dread. 80

" What if indignant fhe decreafe my train

" More than *Latona's* number will remain ?

" Then hence, ye *Theban* dames, hence hafte

    " away,

" Nor longer off'rings to *Latona* pay ?

" Regard the orders of *Amphion's* fpoufe,   85

" And take the leaves of laurel from your brows."

Niobe fpoke.   The *Theban* maids obey'd,

Their brows unbound, and left the rights un-

    paid.

The angry goddefs heard, then filence broke

On *Cynthus'* fummit, and indignant fpoke;   90

        " *Phœbus!*

" *Phœbus!* behold, thy mother in difgrace,

" Who to no goddefs yields the prior place

" Except to *Juno's* felf, who reigns above,

" The fpoufe and fifter of the thund'ring *Jove.*

" *Niobe* fprung from *Tantalus* infpires   95

" Each *Theban* bofom with rebellious fires,

" No reafon her imperious temper quells,

" But all her father in her tongue rebels,

" Wrap her own fons for her blafpheming breath,

" *Apollo!* wrap them in the fhades of death "   100

Latona ceas'd, and ardent thus replies,

The God, whofe glory decks th' expanded fkies.

" Ceafe thy complaints, mine be the tafk af-
          " fign'd

" To punifh pride, and fcourge the rebel mind."

This *Phœbe* join'd.—They wing their inftant
          flight;   - 105

Thebes trembled as th' immortal pow'rs alight.

With clouds incompafs'd glorious *Phœbus*
          ftands;

The feather'd vengeance quiv'ring in his hands.

Near

Near *Cadmus'* walls a plain extended lay,
Where *Thebes'* young princes pafs'd in fport the
    day :   110
There the bold courfers bounded o'er the plains,
While their great mafters held the golden reins.
Ifmenus firft the racing paftime led,
And rul'd the fury of his flying fteed.
" Ah me," he fudden cries, with fhrieking
    breath,   115
While in his breaft he feels the fhaft of death ;
He drops the bridle on his courfer's mane,
Before his eyes in fhadows fwims the plain,
He, the firft-born of great *Amphion's* bed,
Was ftruck the firft, firft mingled with the
    dead.   120

Then didft thou, *Sipylus,* the language hear
Of fate portentous whiftling in the air :
As when th' impending ftorm the failor fees
He fpreads his canvas to the fav'ring breeze,

              So.

So to thine horse thou gav'st the golden reins, 125
Gav'st him to rush impetuous o'er the plains.
But ah! a fatal shaft from *Phœbus*' hand
Smites through thy neck, and sinks thee on the
  sand.

Two other brothers were at wrestling found,
And in their pastime claspt each other round: 130
A shaft that instant from *Apollo's* hand
Transfixt them both, and stretcht them on the
  sand:
Together they their cruel fate bemoan'd,
Together languish'd, and together groan'd.
Together too th' unbodied spirits fled, 135
And sought the gloomy mansions of the dead.

Alphenor saw, and trembling at the view,
Beat his torn breast, that chang'd its snowy hue.
He flies to raise them in a kind embrace,
A brother's fondness triumphs in his face: 140
Alphenor fails in this fraternal deed,
A dart dispatch'd him (so the fates decreed.)
                                    Soon

Soon as the arrow left the deadly wound,
His iffuing entrails fmoak'd upon the ground.

What woes on blooming *Damafichon* wait! 145
His fighs portend his near impending fate.
Juft where the well-made leg begins to be, .
And the foft finews form the fupple knee,
The youth fore wounded by the *Delian* god
Attempts t' extract the crime-avenging rod, 150
But, whilft he ftrives the will of fate t' avert,
Divine *Apollo* fends a fecond dart,
Swift thro' his throat the feather'd mifchief flies,
Bereft of fenfe, he drops his head, and dies.

Young *Ilioneus*, the laft, directs his pray'r, 155
And cries, "My life, ye gods celeftial! fpare."
Apollo heard, and pity touch'd his heart,
But ah! too late, for he had fent the dart:
Thou too, O *Ilioneus*, are doom'd to fall,
The fates refufe that arrow to recal. 160

On

On the swift wings of ever-flying *Fame*
To *Cadmus'* palace soon the tidings came .
Niobe heard, and with indignant eyes
She thus exprefs'd her anger and furprize :
" Why is fuch privilege to them allow'd ?   165
" Why thus infulted by the *Delian* god ?
" Dwells there fuch mifchief in the pow'rs above ?
" Why fleeps the vengeance of immortal *Jove* ?"
For now *Amphion* too, with grief opprefs'd,
Had plung'd the deadly dagger in his breaft. 170
Niobe now, lefs haughty than before,
With lofty head directs her fteps no more.
She, who late told her pedigree divine,
And drove the *Thebans* from *Latona's* fhrine,
How ftrangely chang'd !——yet beautiful in
     woe,   175
She weeps, nor weeps unpity'd by the foe
On each pale corfe the wretched mother fpread
Lay overwhelm'd with grief, and kifs'd her dead,
Then rais'd her arms, and thus, in accents flow,
" Be fated cruel *Goddefs* ! with my woe ,   180
                                            " If

" If I've offended, let thefe ftreaming eyes,

" And let this fev'nfold funeral fuffice :

" Ah ! take this wretched life you deign'd to fave,

" With them I too am carried to the grave.

" Rejoice triumphant, my victorious foe,   185

" But fhow the caufe from whence your triumphs

    " flow ?

" Tho' I unhappy mourn thefe children flain,

" Yet greater numbers to my lot remain."

She ceas'd, the bow ftring twang'd with awful

    found,

Which ftruck with terror all th' affembly round,

Except the queen, who ftood unmov'd alone,

By her diftreffes more prefumptuous grown.

Near the pale corfes ftood their fifters fair

In fable veftures and difhevell'd hair ;

One, while fhe draws the fatal fhaft away,   195

Faints, falls, and fickens at the light of day.

To footh her mother, lo ! another flies,

And blames the fury of inclement fkies,

And, while her words a filial pity fhow,

Struck dumb——indignant feeks the fhades

    below.   200

                                  Now

Now from the fatal place another flies,

Falls in her flight, and languishes, and dies

Another on her sister drops in death,

A fifth in trembling terrors yields her breath,

While the sixth seeks some gloomy cave in
     vain,   205

Struck with the rest, and mingl'd with the slain.

One only daughter lives, and she the least,

The queen close clasp'd the daughter to her breast:

" Ye heav'nly pow'rs, ah spare me one," she cry'd,

" Ah! spare me one," the vocal hills reply'd: 210

In vain she begs, the Fates her suit deny,

In her embrace she sees her daughter die

  * " The queen of all her family bereft,

" Without or husband, son, or daughter left,

" Grew stupid at the shock.   The passing air 215

" Made no impression on her stiff'ning hair.

* This Verse to the End is the Work of another Hand.

                          " The

" The blood forfook her face   amidft the flood
" Pour'd from her cheeks, quite fix'd her eye balls
 " ftood
" Her tongue, her palate both obdurate grew,
" Her curdled veins no longer motion knew , 220
" The ufe of neck, and arms, and feet was gone,
" And ev'n her bowels hard'ned into ftone:
" A marble ftatue now the queen appears,
" But from the marble fteal the filent tears."

P   To

To S. M. a young *African* Painter, on seeing his Works.

TO show the lab'ring bosom's deep intent,
　　And thought in living characters to paint,
When first thy pencil did those beauties give,
And breathing figures learnt from thee to live,
How did those prospects give my soul delight,　5
A new creation rushing on my sight?
Still, wond'rous youth! each noble path pursue,
On deathless glories fix thine ardent view:
Still may the painter's and the poet's fire
To aid thy pencil, and thy verse conspire!　　10
And may the charms of each seraphic theme
Conduct thy footsteps to immortal fame!
High to the blisful wonders of the skies
Elate thy soul, and raise thy wishful eyes.
Thrice happy, when exalted to survey　　15
That splendid city, crown'd with endless day,
Whose twice six gates on radiant hinges ring:
Celestial *Salem* blooms in endless spring.

Calm

Calm and ferene thy moments glide along,
And may the mufe infpire each future fong !   20
Still, with the fweets of contemplation blefs'd,
May peace with balmy wings your foul inveft !
But when thefe fhades of time are chas'd away,
And darknefs ends in everlafting day,
On what feraphic pinions fhall we move,   25
And view the landfcapes in the realms above ?
There fhall thy tongue in heav'nly murmurs flow,
And there my mufe with heav'nly tranfport glow :
No more to tell of *Damon's* tender fighs,
Or rifing radiance of *Aurora's* eyes,   30
For nobler themes demand a nobler ftrain,
And purer language on th' ethereal plain.
Ceafe, gentle mufe ! the folemn gloom of night
Now fteals the fair creation from my fight.

P 2   To

To His Honour the Lieutenant-Governor, on the
Death of his Lady. *March* 24, 1773

ALL-conquering Death! by thy resistless
  pow'r,
Hope's tow'ring plumage falls to rise no more!
Or, scenes terrestrial how the glories fly,
Forget their splendors; and submit to die !
Who ere escap'd thee; but the saint * of old   5
Beyond the flood in sacred annals told,
And the great sage, † whom fiery courses drew
To heav'n's bright portals from *Elisha's* view;
Wond'ring he gaz'd at the refulgent ear,
Then snatch'd the mantle floating on the air.   10
From Death these only could exemption boast,
And without dying gain'd th' immortal coast.
Not falling millions sate the tyrant's mind,
Nor can the victor's progress be confin'd.
But cease thy strife with *Death*, fond *Nature*,
  cease.   15
He leads the *virtuous* to the realms of peace,

  * T.   * Enoch   † Elijah.

                                                 His

His to conduct to the immortal plains,
Where heav'n's Supreme in blifs and glory reigns.

There fits, illuftrious Sir, thy beauteous fpoufe;
A gem-blaz'd circle beaming on her brows   20
Hail'd with acclaim among the heav'nly choirs,
Her foul new-kindling with feraphic fires,
To notes divine fhe tunes the vocal ftrings,
While heav'n's high concave with the mufic rings.
Virtue's rewards can mortal pencil paint?   25
No—all defcriptive arts, and eloquence are faint,
Nor canft thou, *Oliver*, affent refufe
To heav'nly tidings from the *Afric* mufe.

As foon may change thy laws, eternal *fate*,
As the faint mils the glories I relate,   30
Or her *Benevolence* forgotten lie,
Which wip'd the trick'ling tear from *Mis'ry's* eye.
Whene'er the adverfe winds were known to blow,
When lofs to lofs * enfu'd, and woe to woe,

---

* Three amiable Daughters who died when juft arrived to
            Womens Eftate.

Calm

Calm and serene beneath her father's hand   35
She sat resign'd to the divine command.

No longer then, great Sir, her death deplore,
And let us hear the mournful sigh no more,
Restrain the sorrow streaming from thine eye,
Be all thy future moments crown'd with joy !   40
Nor let thy wishes be to earth confin'd,
But soaring high pursue th' unbodied mind
Forgive the muse, forgive th' advent'rous lays,
That fain thy soul to heav'nly scenes would raise.

A Farewel

A Farewel to AMERICA   To Mrs S. W.

I.

ADIEU, *New-England's* fmiling meads,
    Adieu, the flow'ry plain ·
I leave thine op'ning charms, O fpring,
    And tempt the roaring main.

II.

In vain for me the flow'rets rife,   5
    And boaft their gaudy pride,
While here beneath the northern fkies
    I mourn for *health* deny'd.

III.

Celeftial maid of rofy hue,
    O let me feel thy reign !   10
I languifh till thy face I view,
    Thy vanifh'd joys regain.

IV. *Sufannah*

IV.

Susannab mourns, nor can I bear
    To see the cryftal fhow'r,
Or mark the tender falling tear   15
    At fad departure's hour;

V.

Not unregarding can I fee
    Her foul with grief opprest·
But let no fighs, no groans for me,
    Steal from her penfive breaft.   20

VI.

In vain the feather'd warblers fing,
    In vain the garden blooms,
And on the bofom of the fpring
    Breathes out her fweet perfumes,

VII.

While for *Britannia*'s diftant fhore   25
    We fweep the liquid plain,
And with aftonifh'd eyes explore
    The wide-extended main.

VIII. Lo!

VIII.

Lo! *Health* appears! celeftial dame !
  Complacent and ferene,
With *Hebe*'s mantle o'er her Frame,   30
  With foul-delighting mein.

IX.

To mark the vale where *London* lies
  With mifty vapours crown'd,
Which cloud *Aurora*'s thoufand dyes;   35
  And veil her charms around,

X

Why, *Phœbus*, moves thy car fo flow ?
  So flow thy rifing ray ?
Give us the famous town to view,
  Thou glorious king of day !   40

XI.

For thee, *Britannia*, I refign
  New-England's fmiling fields ;
To view again her charms divine,
  What joy the profpect yields !

Q   XII. But

XII.

But thou ! Temptation hence away,   45
  With all thy fatal train
Not once feduce my foul away,
  By thine enchanting ftrain.

XIII.

Thrice happy they, whofe heav'nly fhield
  Secures their fouls from harms,   50
And fell *Temptation* on the field
  Of all its pow'r difarms !

Bofton, May 7, 1773.

A REBUS,

A REBUS, by *I. B.*

I.

A BIRD delicious to the tafte,
   On which an army once did feaft,
  Sent by an hand unfeen;
A creature of the horned race,
Which *Britain's* royal ftandards grace;   5
  A gem of vivid green;

II.

A town of gaiety and fport,
Where beaux and beauteous nymphs refort,
  And gallantry doth reign,
A *Dardan* hero fam'd of old   10
For youth and beauty, as we're told,
  And by a monarch flain;

III.

A peer of popular applaufe,
Who doth our violated laws,
  And grievances proclaim.   15
Th' initials fhow a vanquifh'd town,
That adds frefh glory and renown
  To old *Britannia's* fame.

Q 2   An

An ANSWER to the *Rebus*, by the Author of these
POEMS.

THE poet asks, and *Phillis* can't refuse
To shew th'obedience of the Infant muse.
She knows the *Quail* of most inviting taste
Fed *Israel's* army in the dreary waste;
And what's on *Britain's* royal standard borne, 5
But the tall, graceful, rampant *Unicorn?*
The *Emerold* with a vivid verdure glows
Among the gems which regal crowns compose;
Boston's a town, polite and debonair,
To which the beaux and beauteous nymphs repair,
Each *Helen* strikes the mind with sweet surprise,
While living lightning flashes from her eyes.
See young *Euphorbus* of the *Dardan* line
By *Menelaus'* hand to death resign :
The well known peer of popular applause
Is C—m zealous to support our laws.
    Quebec now vanquish'd must obey,
    She too must annual tribute pay
    To *Britain* of immortal fame,
    And add new glory to her name.   20

F I N I S.

CONTENTS.

On

C O N T E N T S.

On

CONTENTS.

Lately Published in 2 vols Twelves, *(Price* 5s *sewed,)*

THE
M E M O I R S
OF
MISS W I L L I A M S.

A

HISTORY FOUNDED ON FACTS

BY A. B***,

LONDON Printed for E. JOHNSON, in Ave Mary Lane; and A. BELL, near the SARACEN'S HEAD, ALDGATE

WRITTEN *by the same* AUTHOR,

Shortly will be published, (*in a neat Pocket Volume*)

THE
CHURCH-MEMBER's DIRECTORY,
OR,
EVERY CHRISTIAN's COMPANION

Designed for the Use of such as have engaged in a solemn Connection with CHRIST's Visible Church.

WHEREIN

The Duties of that high Relation are considered, both in a religious and moral Point of View

Let every one that nameth the name of Christ depart from iniquity. 2 Tim. Chap 11 v 19

TOGETHER WITH

An ADDRESS to those who have an Intention of entering upon that important Character.

For which of you intending to build a tower, sitteth not down first and counteth the cost, whether he have sufficient *to finish it?*

Lest haply after he hath laid the foundation, and is not able to finish it, all that behold it, begin to mock him.

Saying, This man began to build, and was not able to finish.

Luke Chap. xiv. Ver. 28, 29, 30.

CPSIA information can be obtained
at www.ICGtesting.com
Printed in the USA
LVHW081923040123
736465LV00004B/138